SPIRITUAL WARFARE

GROUP BIBLE STUDY

WRITTEN BY Frank Lattimore

Spiritual Warfare: Group Bible Study
Written by Frank Lattimore

Requests for information should be sent to:
Warner Press Inc.
P.O. Box 2499
Anderson, IN 46018
www.warnerpress.org

Kevin Stiffler • Editor
S. Katie Miller • Layout & Design

CONTENTS

The Warner Press *Relevance* Group Bible Studies provide intriguing examinations of topics using the whole of the Scriptures. The guides incorporate various stories and activities to introduce and apply the subject matter, with a Bible study component at the heart of each session. Our goal is to show life-long believers and those new to the faith how to know the Lord intimately while encouraging them to step out and join him in his work with miraculous results.

These flexible studies are ideal for any setting. We know that time is a valuable commodity in today's society, and that's why each book consists of five or six short lessons intended to meet the group's scheduling needs.

L1

In the Beginning: The War Begins

Genesis 2:15—3:24; Luke 10:18; John 10:10

Main Point

It's important to know what spiritual warfare is, to understand its origins and where it takes place, while also understanding the difference between it and the curse under which all of humankind lives.

Background

Spiritual warfare can be defined as the ongoing battle against a demonic enemy attempting to subvert human relationships with God. Living in a physical world, most of humanity believes that the things we observe visually and audibly are all that exist. But the Bible informs us of another realm, equally as real and sometimes just as observable.

Who is involved in spiritual warfare?

1. The Trinity—God the Father, Son, and Holy Spirit—present everywhere, all-knowing, all-powerful, plus legions of angels.
2. Satan and demons (a.k.a. the enemy)—fallen angels that are finite in knowledge and power.
3. Humankind—much more finite in knowledge and power than the enemy.

Realizing There Is an Enemy

In the garden of Eden, Adam and Eve had a day of grave realization. It came after being deceived by the father of lies—Satan—causing all of creation to fall under a curse. Satan's deception: *Did God really say that? God's not telling the whole truth. You can have—and be—more.*

We have a tendency to lay blame on Adam and Eve for the "curse"—the hell-to-pay separation of humankind from God—that resulted from their sin. But any of us would have been the cause if we had been the first ones tempted and deceived. The first couple came to understand that they had an enemy who was going to battle for humankind's destruction.

When and how did you first become aware that you live in a world submerged in a spiritual war?

____

____

____

____

How does this knowledge shape your view on the chaos that exists in our world?

____

____

____

As a Christian, what do you believe are the primary reasons the enemy wants to keep you from being aware of and involved in the spiritual conflicts that surround us?

In the children's book *The Lion, the Witch and the Wardrobe* by C. S. Lewis, Peter, Susan, Edmund, and Lucy Pevensie enter the snowy country of Narnia through a magical wardrobe, only to find that it's "always winter, but never Christmas." The world they've entered doesn't make sense—it lacks context—until they encounter Mr. and Mrs. Beaver, who explain how the ruling White Witch cursed the land with her evil power and took dominion over it. But rumors persist that Aslan, the rightful king, is on the move to take it back.

I. Read Genesis 2:15–25.

God placed Adam in a perfect place with specific purpose. And he gave Adam the very first command, to "not eat from the tree of the knowledge of good and evil" (v 17). Would you have been curious about why the tree was given its name? Might it have troubled you to not understand? Why or why not?

We don't know about Adam's thought processes or whether he was curious about the name of that tree, but it seems he was okay with God's command because he didn't question it. What *may* have been the reason(s) Adam chose not to question God about either the tree's name or his command not to eat from it?

God's account of the Fall—especially how sin led to internal shame within humanity—must have been both strange and eye-opening to the writer of Genesis. Before the Fall, Adam and Eve lived their lives naked and didn't feel or understand shame. What do you believe is significant about this?

II. Read Genesis 3:1–19.

In verse 1, when the serpent asked Eve, "Did God really say…?", doubt began spinning in her head, especially since she wasn't the one who heard God speak the command. Describe a time when you were challenged about something you believed God's Word said. How did that challenge play on your mind?

In verses 2–3, we find that Adam had accurately conveyed to Eve what must not be done and why. But in verse 4, the serpent—the devil or Satan—challenged that. Since Eve didn't exist when Adam was given the command, proof of it eluded her. When have you found yourself questioning a "voice" in your mind? Could such a voice ever be from an unseen, outside influence? Explain.

Even though Adam had accurately shared God's commandment with Eve, he failed by not protecting her when she was deceived by the serpent. We don't know why Adam accepted the fruit from Eve and ate, but he could have stopped the whole event. As a result, sin caused shame, redefining their nakedness. Being naked equates to being exposed. How has being exposed because of sin caused you shame?

In verses 12–19, Adam blamed Eve and Eve blamed the serpent—everyone was "passing the buck." God, however, put an end to their blame game by holding all three to account. All were heavily punished, though the devil's ultimate punishment was still to come.

III. Read Genesis 3:20–24.

Thank God for verse 21! After shedding the blood of an innocent animal to make clothing from its skin, God covered both Eve and Adam, proving that he still loved them. Earlier that day, they had both been exposed—physically and spiritually—but then it all got covered. Our Creator performed a similar act for *us*. How and why?

Why is it important that we understand original sin—the creation-corrupting very first sin—and have context for the condition of the world in which we now live?

Based on Genesis 3, what are some attributes of our enemy?

Who stands accountable for our cursed world? Is it the devil, is it Adam and Eve, or is it someone or something else? Why do you say so?

Understanding original sin clears up a lot of confusion about life and God. After that awful day, everything was different: thorns, death, sickness, murderous hearts, self-gratification of every sort, the destruction of people's lives—and hell, both here on earth and in the everlasting that follows. Imagine if we didn't know about the fall of creation—the curse. Imagine if God had not provided this back-story for us in his Word. Where would that have left us? It would have left us with a lot of reasons to cry out, "God, why?!"

How do you think understanding original sin will help you view God differently when troubling times occur in your life?

Does reflecting on the things that have happened on earth since the curse give you a new perspective about our enemy? If so, how does it change things in your heart and mind?

IV. Read Luke 10:18 and John 10:10.

Who is Satan? It's important to know, because this, too, will help with understanding what's going on in the world around us. Jesus said, "I saw Satan fall like lightning from heaven." Satan, the devil, was the greatest of all of God's created beings, powerful and glorious. He committed insurrection, but it failed. Since that day, there has been vengeance dominating Satan's mind, with legions of demons following his lead. His desire is to get as many of God's image-bearers as possible to end up in hell with him. This is where spiritual warfare had its beginning, but according to the Scriptures, God gets to determine where it all ends.

We who know Jesus as Lord get to look forward to victory, and we'll get to rejoice over Satan's defeat. What does this realization stir within you?

According to the Scriptures, the day is coming when humankind will once again get to live in paradise with God, without sin and all the brokenness that has come with it. Just imagine a pristine creation with no earthquakes, tornadoes, or hurricanes. It will be a place of peace, joy, purpose, laughter, and great relationships. Every one of us will personally know Jesus face-to-face. And the "father of lies" will be thrown into the lake of fire forever. What began with him fooling us into believing we could "be like God" will end with him never being able to mess with anyone ever again.

How will combining your knowledge of original sin with an understanding of our future in paradise shape your attitude toward the problems and complexities of living on earth today?

Closing Prayer

Father, while we don't enjoy the idea that we've got to spend the rest of our days on this side of heaven living under the curse, we do appreciate that you loved us enough to share the account that details why this world is the way it is. Please help us to keep original sin in mind when we witness and experience sickness, pain, hate, and so many other broken features of this world. Help us to be mindful of the enemy and his continued role in trying to keep humankind blind to what's really going on. In Jesus' name, Amen.■

L2

Protection: Is It God's Responsibility?

Ezekiel 28:11–17; Isaiah 14:12–17; Revelation 12:3–13; 2 Corinthians 10:3–6;

1 Corinthians 10:13; Romans 8:31–39

Main Point

We know from the Scriptures that God is all-knowing (omniscient), everywhere at the same time (omnipresent), and all-powerful (omnipotent), but we are also made aware that God calls us to an active role *with him* to use spiritual weaponry to defend ourselves, defend others, and make heaven full.

Background

The enemy is a very real and present danger. If Satan had his way, every single Christian would be wiped off the planet so he could focus on having "fun" with all those he's steering toward hell. The Book of Job details how he seems to take pleasure in applying emotional and physical duress. Maybe we are in a more dangerous situation than we could have ever imagined. And maybe we're supposed to be an integral part of the solution.

Fight, Flight, or Ignore?

In the famed Christian allegorical poem *The Faerie Queene* by Edmund Spenser, Redcrosse Knight encounters a dragon symbolizing the apex of all sin and evil. The knight sees the overwhelming size and strength of the greatest of his enemies, a creature embodying sin and producing internal fears, both of which he must learn to defeat. Such is the case with every one of us who must contend with our unseen foe.

The Bible makes it clear that there is a worldwide war taking place in the spirit realm. How active do you believe Satan and his demons are in modern society? Why?

____

____

How do you respond to the idea of spiritual warfare? Does it cause dread? If so, why? If not, why not? How does this type of warfare currently play a role in your life as a Christian?

____

____

____

Have you ever been involved in spiritual battles in the past? If so, what was it like for you?

____

____

____

I. Read Ezekiel 28:11–17; Isaiah 14:12–17; and Revelation 12:3–13.

Why do we need protection, and what do we need to know about our adversaries, Satan and his demons? We learn from these passages that after Satan—the former archangel called "guardian cherub," "morning star," and "son of the dawn"—was defeated in his attempt to take over God's throne and was cast out of heaven.

Based on Revelation 12:4, the dragon's (Satan's) tail "swept a third of the stars out of the sky and flung them to the earth." What do you believe these "stars" represent?

____

____

____

____

____

____

Because Satan and his demons are relegated to a forthcoming fiery eternity, they are bent on bringing the same hellish destruction upon as many of God's image-bearers as possible. How do you view non-Christians who live within your sphere of influence? How motivated are you to introduce as many people to Christ as possible? Why?

____

____

____

____

II. Read 2 Corinthians 10:3–6.

There are many Old Testament verses used by Christians to proclaim that the Lord will fight our battles for us. However, the popular "warfare" verses—promises made by God—pertain to specific physical human-on-human conflicts. (If you're interested, here are a few of the most widely used today: Deut 20:4, Ps 44:5, Jer 1:19.)

It's not until we read the New Testament that we see descriptions of humankind-involved *spiritual* warfare. Spiritual usage of the words *oppressed* and *possessed* are introduced in the Book of Matthew, as is the word *demon*. In the Old Testament, we gain insight into the origins and workings of Satan, but it's only in the New Testament that we learn about our authority to overcome him and his demonic war machine.

In the spirit realm, two aspects of our battles are vital: protecting ourselves and fighting for others. While it's easy to understand why we need to be protected from the enemy's arguments and attacks, based on 2 Corinthians 10:4–5, why do you believe it's important that Christians engage the enemy on behalf of both believers and non-believers?

____

____

____

____

____

____

The statements of 2 Corinthians 10:4–5 cannot be overstated; spiritual attacks take place in the physical and spiritual realms, but they also take place within the *mind*. Sometimes troubling thoughts may be whispers from the enemy. How does this bring clarity to troubling thoughts you may have battled?

In future lessons, the focus will be on various forms of weaponry made available to us that we are called to use. If weaponry is provided to you by Christ, can you argue that God alone is responsible for your protection and the protection of others? Explain.

Do you believe that just praying for someone (or yourself) is sufficient for engaging in spiritual warfare? Why or why not?

III. Read 1 Corinthians 10:13.

Nowhere in the Bible does it say, "God won't allow more to happen to you than you can handle." That's a deceitful twisting of the Scriptures. People who believe this have been set up for a fall by the enemy. What God actually promised is that there will be no *temptation* greater than you can overcome, with the added promise, "He will also provide a way out so that you can endure it."

Twisting the Scriptures is one specialty of the enemy. Another is creating "quotes" that sound like they come from the Bible. Have you ever become hurt or mentally disillusioned because of someone's mishandling of the Scriptures? How can you defeat this type of spiritual attack?

____

____

____

What are some important reasons why God might allow painful circumstances—that can't be handled on your own—to enter your life and the lives of others?

____

____

____

IV. Read Romans 8:31–39.

Your protection is your responsibility—*and* God's. He's the provider of everything we need, from "ways out" of temptation to the vast array of weaponry necessary for defeating the enemy's attacks against us—and others.

After all, we are "soldiers" and "more than conquerors" because of God's active role in our lives.

Within this passage, what is the statement made by the apostle Paul that strikes you the most? Why?

___

___

___

Knowing God's love and his desire for intimacy, how much time do you spend in your Bible? Do you typically just read it, or do you deliberately research and study its multiple topics? What might need to change in this area?

___

___

___

Closing Prayer

Father, thank you for not leaving us weaponless. We're grateful that we can link arms with you for both our protection and the protection of those you'll put in our paths in the future. Help us to learn from your Word personally, rather than merely being told what it says. And help us—ones you call "more than conquerors"—to grow in courage and responsibility as soldiers of your Kingdom. In Jesus' name, Amen.■

L3

The Enemy Hates You and Your Confidence

1 Corinthians 16:13; Romans 8:1; 2 Timothy 1:7; Ephesians 4:30; 1 Samuel 17

Main Point

In an attempt to make you ineffective in your Christian walk, the enemy strives to attack the confidence you have in your salvation and in your role as a warrior for the kingdom of Christ, but if you understand key statements in the Scriptures, you need not doubt.

Background

If there is one thing you can count on after becoming a Christian, it's the horrible doubt—whether brief or perpetual—that you can maintain your salvation. In fact, the enemy wants you to earnestly believe that God's grace has limits.

Before you were saved, the enemy wanted you to believe that you were okay the way you were, not needing that "Jesus stuff." And since your salvation, the enemy's goal has been to cast doubt on your redemption and your worthiness to be used for the cause of Christ, especially after committing additional sins.

When Sin and the Enemy Make You Feel Unworthy

When you're depressed or filled with despair—especially after a big spiritual fail—hope and assurance feel vanquished, and self-pity becomes the governing principle. In other words, everyday life becomes *you* thinking primarily about *you*. Your attention is removed from Kingdom-focused productivity. It's time to open the Word of God, because it's likely you're under attack. You're now being ruled by something other than God's Spirit: whispers from the enemy about God's abandonment and the loss of your salvation. Even if you remain confident that you're going to heaven, the enemy will try a different tack: "You think God still wants to use you after *that*?"

Have you ever doubted your salvation because of some sort of personal failure? If so, describe the experience. How long did that feeling last?

If the sins of all the people who have ever lived—and ever will live—were carried by Jesus on the cross, how many of your future sins—as a Christian—would it take to cast you back into a spiritually unredeemed state?

What do Billy Graham, Charles Colson, Charlotte Elliot (the writer of the hymn "Just as I Am"), Martin Luther, John Bunyan, missionaries Lottie Moon and Elizabeth Elliot, and Charles Spurgeon all have in common?

Every one of these great men and women of God believed, at points in their Christian walk, that they may have lost their salvation. Why? Because of failures—*as Christians*—believing they may have crossed a line. But *what* line?

I. **Read** 1 Corinthians 16:13.

As Paul wrapped up this letter to Christians in Corinth, he was speaking about people of interest to the church. But then he interrupted his flow and made a statement that seemed to pull from Joshua 1:9, which reads, "Have I not commanded you? Be strong and courageous. Do not be afraid; do not be discouraged, for the Lord your God will be with you wherever you go." But Paul began with, "Be on your guard." What does that warning mean to you?

____

____

____

II. **Read** Romans 8:1; 2 Timothy 1:7; and Ephesians 4:30.

Romans 8:1 states, "There is now no condemnation for those who are in Christ Jesus." In what grammatical tense is this verse written: past, present, or future? Why is the tense important?

____

____

____

The moment you accepted Jesus as your Savior, these verses went into effect. Here's how Romans 8:1 is relevant. Read it again with inserted context:

> Once you become a Christian, *there is no longer any* condemnation for future sins *because* you are *in* Christ Jesus.

Jesus, in his own words, promised that "no one," including the enemy, will be able to snatch you from the Father's hand (John 10:28–29). The Scriptures also state that God will never leave or forsake you (Heb 13:5). You might choose to walk away from God, but he will not abandon you because of your mistakes. Forgiveness today means flawlessness the day we leave earth for heaven.

After God's mightiest creature—the archangel we now know as Satan—failed in his revolt against the throne of God, he was cast out of heaven. The name Satan has two interchangeable interpretations: *adversary* and *slanderer*. Revelation 12:10 assigns him this description: "the accuser of our brothers and sisters, who accuses them before our God day and night." We all know those accusations—the ones for failure to stand against temptation. How do accusations from the enemy mess with your mind and emotions?

____

____

____

Jesus called Satan "the father of lies" (John 8:44). Therefore, you can reliably believe the opposite of the despair you may feel after committing a sin, because "there is now no condemnation for those who are in Christ Jesus." This is not permission to sin, mind you, as sin is still self-harm and causes the Holy Spirit who lives in you to grieve. Your remorse for an act of a sin is healthy and leads to repentance.

Now, keeping in mind Jesus' description of Satan, would your enemy waste his time speaking condemnation to you if you were already—once again—

condemned by God? Why would Satan try to make you feel condemned in the midst of your rock-solid salvation?

If the enemy is successful at getting you to fear the loss of your salvation and live in shame, you'll be sabotaged and sidelined. How do Romans 8:1 and 2 Timothy 1:7 speak to you when you read them one after the other?

How can confidence in your salvation help you resist the attacks of the enemy?

III. Read 1 Samuel 17.

The shepherd boy David, youngest of the sons of Jesse, was sent out by his father to the battle between the armies of Israel and Philistia. Jesse wanted to provide some food for his sons, but he also sought details about the battle and the health of his children. When David arrived, he learned that there had been forty-plus days of inaction between the armies. And he discovered that the reason for the inaction was fear.

King Saul and his army were terrified of a single, imposing Philistine soldier: Goliath, a man whose height approached ten feet. This warrior brandished weapons that normal men wouldn't be effective in using because of their size and weight. Goliath's daily railings against the army of King Saul were deliberate taunts for a single Israelite to come forth to fight him. This would, of course, avoid bloodshed on both sides, but the losing side would become slaves of the other. No one in Israel's ranks of soldiers had the courage to challenge him, despite Saul's promise of great rewards for the killer of Goliath. Hence, the stalemate.

Israel wasn't afraid of a battle. They feared one single accuser and slanderer.

But—along came a shepherd boy with the courage of a man of God in his heart. He questioned his brothers about the situation but was rebuked for being there. David discovered, though, that all the men of the army were lacking two things: courage and confidence.

Then David spoke with the king. He wanted to be the one who went out as Israel's champion, stating that God had been preparing him for this unforeseen contest.

What did David have that no one else in Israel's front lines had? What reasons did he have for believing he could win head-to-head against Goliath?

It's easy to conclude that David's past confrontations with lions and bears gave him the ability to win against Goliath. But there was something that took place in the previous chapter (see 1 Sam 16:1, 13) that may have been all that was needed for him to have the courage and confidence to win. What was it?

All of us as Christians need to be equipped and filled with confidence to win battles against our enemy. All of us are tasked with being prepared and on guard.

How is your confidence in your salvation? Why?

Philippians 1:6 says we should be "confident of this, that he who began a good work in you will carry it on to completion until the day of Christ Jesus." In what area of your spiritual walk are you lacking the most confidence? What can you do to change that?

Closing Prayer

Father, we are flawed human beings. But you call us out to be more than that. Help us to be confident in the calling and purposes you have for us—within a body of believers and as individuals. You've promised that we can do what you ask through Christ who provides his strength. Help us to grow in knowledge, skill, and confidence in our right-standing with you so we can defend ourselves and those around us who may be threatened by the enemy. In Jesus' name, Amen. ■

CARLOS

L4

We Need Weaponry

2 Corinthians 10:3–5; Ephesians 6:10–18; 2 Corinthians 6:1–10

Main Point

Spiritual warfare is exactly what it sounds like: the use of spiritual weaponry to protect ourselves (and others), pushing back against a relentless, unseen enemy that wants to keep the lost separated from God and the found ineffective for the Kingdom.

Background

Our world is filled with mischief and chaos. Some of it comes from our own sinful appetites, but there is also that which comes from an unseen, unrelenting enemy. The Scriptures wouldn't open our eyes to spiritual weaponry if it were not for our use. And just as our enemy is unseen, so are the weapons supplied to us (with the exception of the Word of God), but they are no less real, powerful, and needed for the advancement of the kingdom of God than the physical weapons used in physical battles. We believers must learn how to use them productively in the war that daily surrounds us. But that means we must also learn about the goals and tactics of the enemy.

A Directive to Participate

Satan and his horde of demons will do everything in their power to defeat us physically, emotionally, mentally, and spiritually. But God is also the supplier of everything we need to be victorious when we—or those we care about—are attacked. Jesus is the commander-in-chief of all the forces of heaven, and there have been an unknown number of times when they've defended us without us even knowing. At the same time, we also must identify attacks and take up our own weaponry to engage in battle. So, while Jesus certainly delights in being our hero, he also desires to be our congratulator with a "Well done!"

Distinguishing between the problems we have resulting from the fall and those resulting from spiritual attacks isn't always easy. Attacks from the enemy can come in many different forms: fear, depression, heaviness, headaches, nightmares, etc. But any of these could also have situational, environmental, or chemical causes. The great thing is that engaging in spiritual warfare even when there isn't enemy involvement won't do any harm.

How does the idea of engaging a spiritual enemy make you feel? What, if any, concerns do you have?

What are some ways spiritual warfare may be an aid to your life and for the defense of another individual?

Have there been any situations in which you have engaged in spiritual warfare? If so, briefly describe them.

When armies of different nations engage in battle, they do so having already done their best to prepare. They fully know and understand their weapons, and they wear flak jackets, helmets, combat boots, and sometimes personal protective equipment (PPE) for threats such as chemical weapons. They understand that all of these things work in concert to protect them as individuals and as a unit. Some of their equipment, though, is provided to dispense harm to the opposition.

I. Read 2 Corinthians 10:3–5.

Verses 3–4 make it clear that there are differences between the wars and weaponry of the physical realm and the war and weaponry of the spirit realm. What do you believe is the primary distinction between them?

In verse 4, we find an interesting insight into the usage of our weapons. We already know that a weapon not wielded is useless. But even a weapon held in one's hand must be backed by strength in order to inflict damage on an enemy combatant. What insight does this verse provide?

II. Read Ephesians 6:10–18.

Paul wrote the Book of Ephesians to a growing church. It's not a letter of rebuke; it's more a book of praise, encouragement, and admonishment. He was addressing people who were listening and willing to make changes. This was a church that wanted to extend love and help God's people. They were supporting the church's mission to spread the gospel throughout the world. Maybe this is why Paul couldn't end his letter without making them aware of their enemy and how to fight back.

According to verses 10–12, we humans live in a physical world intermingled with a spirit world in which skirmishes, battles, and an overarching war are being fought. How might this alter your mindset toward some future life challenges? How about challenges in the lives of others in your relational sphere?

Maybe because we are prone to wandering off like sheep, Paul directed us twice in this passage to "put on the full armor of God." But why do you think he also used the word *therefore* in verse 13?

Considering the use of the word *struggle* and the repeated usage of the words *against* and *stand* (vv 12–14), what should our perpetual mindset be when it comes to the unseen world that surrounds us?

List the types of weaponry highlighted in Ephesians 6 and indicate how familiar you are with each.

Believers are required to remain prepared for spiritual battle. Do *you* have a responsibility that goes beyond praying for yourself and those having spiritual struggles? If so, what is it (v 18)?

As someone who wants to help the church complete its mission of reaching the lost, what does Ephesians 6:10–18 mean *to* and *for* you?

III. Read 2 Corinthians 6:1–10.

Though we are involved in a very real spiritual war, there may be times in our lives—in our call to serve God—when we find ourselves dealing with physical blows in addition to spiritual ones. We are not promised safety in this life; in fact, Jesus said we would face "trouble" (John 16:33). The apostle Paul certainly had his fill of physical and emotional trouble while fighting his spiritual battles—struggles that might have sidelined many of us. But he persisted because he knew there would be a literal hell to pay for those who did not know Jesus.

When you read this passage, what do you note about the type of weapons Paul wielded? What were they, and how were they gripped?

Why would this specific type of weaponry be needed as opposed to, say, weapons of hate and trickery? What would the benefit be for a Christian to wield this type of weaponry in both hands as opposed to one hand? What principle is being hinted at here?

Regardless of what the scripted Hollywood thrills in movies tell us, going into battle without a plan and without weaponry will always end in defeat or death. But for some reason, many Christians spend their days out in a world at war and don't really think of being "at the mercy" of a merciless enemy.

We are targets. Most of the time, this doesn't result in physical death (at least not in the immediate sense), but it does result in being distracted from God's mission for our lives. People who are in our sphere of influence don't hear the gospel. People who are hurting don't get shown compassion. And people who are looking for answers go to the wrong sources for them.

How willing are you to pick up your provided weaponry and engage an enemy that's fighting to destroy those around you, and why?

Ultimate victory against the enemy happens when someone comes into a saving relationship with Jesus. Whom are you willing to fight for in order that they might receive this victory?

Closing Prayer

Father, too often we find ourselves amid chaos and confusion. Sometimes it feels like an attack against us, and sometimes it looks like an attack against someone else. Help us to discern when the enemy is directly involved. Also, remind us to be prepared daily for what we may encounter by putting on the full armor of God and understanding how each component is used—for our protection, for the salvation of the lost, and for direct combat against the enemy. In Jesus' name, Amen.■

L5

The Weapons (and Gear) of Your Warfare

Ephesians 6:10–18

Main Point

True warfare cannot be conducted, let alone won, without weaponry and protection.

Background

Throughout the Old Testament, warfare was physical, resulting in a lot of death and maiming. Things really changed with the New Testament, when Jesus made it clear that there is an *unseen* enemy. The authors of the Book of Acts and the Epistles also shared what was revealed to them about this foe (e.g. 1 Peter 5:8–9). But it was the apostle Paul who taught about the access we have to the weapons required for winning spiritual conflicts.

Instruments of God

In his book *Supernatural: What the Bible Teaches About the Unseen World—and Why It Matters*, author Michael S. Heiser wondered about our influence and effectiveness as instruments of God, which often seem to pale in comparison to those of the apostle Paul. Heiser concluded that Paul had a clear understanding of his life's purpose, and that he believed the power at work behind and within him was greater than the unseen powers at work in this world.

Do you think your work for the Kingdom—sharing the good news about Jesus' death and resurrection—has been hampered in any way by an unseen foe? If so, how?

I. Read Ephesians 6:10–18.

This passage is central to understanding spiritual warfare, so we are visiting it again and focusing specifically on it in this lesson. The text has the distinctive sound of a military commander standing before his troops, admonishing them to be courageous and to perform their best against the enemy they are about to engage. In verse 12, Paul told us to understand who the *real* enemy is. Why?

These verses make it clear that the enemy hordes are organized and dangerous. Their purpose is to beat you down, make you fearful, and keep you unfocused and silent about Christ. How will you respond, and why?

We might classify the different spiritual weapons mentioned in Ephesians 6 as weaponry for protection, weaponry for advancement, or weaponry to vanquish the enemy.

Weaponry for Protection

The Helmet of Salvation

If you are not a true believer in Jesus, bad things can occur during spiritual warfare. For example, Acts 19:13–16 tells us what happened to seven non-Christian sons of a Jewish priest who were trying to drive out demons in Jesus' name. Because they didn't have what we might call "Kevlar helmets of salvation," they were torn up by the enemy. Assurance of your salvation through Jesus alone is essential for any spiritual conflict.

The Breastplate of Righteousness

Ceramic-plate-like chest protection is vital. If the enemy's target is your heart and he is able to attack the core of who you are as a believer, it can make you feel unworthy of being a part of God's mission or even his kingdom. Knowing that God's righteousness is forever embedded within you, despite spiritual stumbles and falls, will help you stand firm against your foe's lies.

The Shield of Faith

According to Hebrews 11:1, "Faith is confidence in what we hope for and assurance about what we do not see." *Confidence.* In Lesson 3, we focused on how the enemy seeks to shatter confidence. Using modern terms, the shield of faith is like a ballistic shield (think of police officers in riot gear). Much like its Roman counterpart, it can be gripped and held in front of you to protect against all sorts of projectiles from the enemy.

So, how is faith gained and grown? Romans 10:17 states, "Faith comes from hearing the message, and the message is heard through the word about Christ." Learning the accounts of those who went before us—from Bible times through today—is important. Hearing and reading how God delivered his followers is an essential faith-developer. When you exercise your faith, you will increase that faith over time. Unused faith is lack of faith.

The Belt of Truth

The Roman uniform "belt" was a skirt-like girdle with leather slats from the waist to just above the knees. It was designed with attachments to hold a sword or dagger, along with the ability to store rations and signaling devices. Today's uniform combat belts are also multi-functional, providing warriors quick access to additional ammunition, a handgun, water, bandages, and other supplies to aid in close-quarter combat and maintain health. From a spiritual perspective, remember that Jesus identified himself as the truth, and his word—God's Word—is always true. Diligent study of the Bible will help you identify false narratives. Your "belt of truth" is essential for effectively scrutinizing the enemy's lies about the foundations of your faith.

Have you ever experienced a spiritual attack? If so, in what form? Were you able to counter it? If so, how?

Weaponry for Advancement

Feet Fitted with Readiness

Without boots (sandals in Roman times), you're going to have a tough time running or walking in war zones. For example, if the Lord directs you to share your testimony and the gospel, and you aren't prepared to march when and where God tells you, you'll likely not do it at all. So, it is good to know your personal testimony to the degree that you can share it without advanced notice. Learn how to share the gospel in the same way. One day you may end up face-to-face with someone who will soon pass away, and maybe you'll be his or her last opportunity to hear about Jesus.

How much of a priority is sharing the gospel for you? Are you prepared? Explain.

Weaponry to Vanquish the Enemy

The Sword of the Spirit

This is the big gun, your spiritual Howitzer or M1 Abrams tank: the Word of God. When it comes to smaller pieces of weaponry such as a handgun, not a whole lot of knowledge is needed, but you won't make much of a dent in the enemy's ranks with them either. For the other, more formidable pieces of offensive weaponry, you must have immersive training, and you've got to read the manufacturers' operation manuals.

After reading the operation manual for complex equipment, you may begin to think you've got the equipment mastered. But reading it one time does not make you an expert gunner or experienced tank operator. No, you've got to keep referring to it, especially when there's something specific about the equipment that you need to master. Such is the case with the content of the Bible. Some subjects in the Scriptures need to be sought out and studied intently for them to become great sources of help—both for you and against the enemy. Not studying your Bible opens the door to injuries.

Spiritual warfare, in almost all cases, should be performed out loud—the *spoken Word*—so the enemy can hear it. You don't wave this sword around in order to vanquish the enemy; you must aggressively *speak* it in the name of Jesus (Mark 16:17; Luke 10:17). Memorize some verses and passages to make them part of your counter-attacks. Force the enemy to hear and acknowledge the authority of God's Word.

Many times, the only way to defeat the enemy is to be unrelenting, overwhelming, and overpowering. The enemy needs to flee, having been injured, making him wish he had never come at you or others you're helping to protect. Your aggressiveness will send a strong message about what will happen if he tries to engage you again.

What difference does it make when we think of the enemy as someone who can be "taught a lesson"?

Spiritual warfare, in the vast majority of cases, is unlikely to become a harrowing experience for you or other Christians with whom you may team up. With that in mind, someone who's seen a positive result from your use of spiritual warfare will most likely perceive a benefit for future uses. Sword wielding can be quickly taught to, learned by, and used by other Christians for their own defense. In the future, these believers may also pass on the same flame.

We have a responsibility to pray for our brothers and sisters in Christ. But what if we know we can do more? How can you take active steps to help other believers learn how to resist and defeat the enemy? How can you come alongside them in their spiritual struggles and do some warfare with them?

____

____

____

____

____

____

Closing Prayer

Father, thank you for aiding us in our protection. We know that, at times, you keep struggles and injury from advancing to our doorsteps. But we are also learning that you've invited us into the struggle so we can know the truth about an unseen army of malice. We pray that we will be effective as both protectors and sharers of the good news about salvation through Jesus. Help us learn how to use this knowledge for the building of your kingdom. In Jesus' name, Amen. ■

L6

Resistance Is Not Futile

Genesis 4:1–8; James 1:13–15; Matthew 6:13; Philippians 4:6–7; Colossians 4:2; Ephesians 6:18; 1 Thessalonians 5:16–18; 1 Peter 5:8–9; James 4:7; Luke 10:17; Proverbs 18:10; Philippians 2:9–10; Mark 16:17; Luke 10:17; Hebrews 4:16

Main Point

Sometimes the enemy is spiritual; sometimes it's the flesh we are fighting, but both can be effectively resisted.

Background

While Ephesians 6 presents our means of effective protection and some very powerful weapons, it does not encapsulate *everything* needed—or useful—for battles. Much of the time, you will not be involved in heavy conflict with an enemy agent. However, the enemy will entice you with mental and visual temptations: things your flesh craves. Giving in to these "whispers" can open the door to confusion, guilt, and demonic oppression. A few preventive measures, though—things that fit nicely into your daily routine—can keep the enemy from wanting to approach you very often.

The Flesh: Not the Enemy, but Close

Let's face it. All the serpent had to do in the garden of Eden was get a single visual temptation to work. After it did, sin entered the world, and corruption immediately followed, including corruption of the heart. Everything needed to perpetuate sin within every heart of every human who would ever live was contained in that original sin.

Your flesh will create its own temptations. And the enemy is certainly willing to intensify them, watching with pleasure as you foster your own downfall.

How often, and in what ways, are you tempted by your flesh to do something the enemy would enjoy watching?

What effective ways have you found to battle the temptations of both your flesh and the enemy?

I. Read Genesis 4:1–8; James 1:13–15; and Matthew 6:13.

Spiritual warfare is not a replacement for doing the necessary hard work of correcting our thought patterns. We are very capable of being our own worst stumbling blocks. Our flesh wants what it wants, whether it's visual, physical, or mental. In these cases, it might not technically be a spiritual warfare situation, but it's certainly still spiritual. For example, there is no indication in the Bible that Satan whispered into the heart of Cain to kill his brother. Instead, the flesh took over in the form of jealousy and anger, then temptation created something in his imagination: *What if there's a way to eliminate Abel?*

According to James 1:14, temptation comes from our own evil desires. Then what happens?

In Genesis 4:7, God, speaking to Cain, provided a single helpful instruction regarding sin. What is it? How is that instruction applicable to our own sin nature?

In Matthew 6:13, Jesus taught us to pray, asking the Father to "lead us not into temptation," which sort of makes it sound like God may want us tempted. A more literal translation—the NIV provides this as a footnote—

indicates that Jesus was saying we should ask God to "lead us not into testing," perhaps of the sort he went through while in the wilderness (Matt 4:1–11). Is this information new to you? If so, how will you use it to pray differently?

____

____

____

II. Read Philippians 4:6–7; Colossians 4:2; Ephesians 6:18; and 1 Thessalonians 5:16–18.

Constant communication with the Lord is incredibly valuable when it comes to conquering the flesh. Who, while having a deep conversational connection with the Father, is likely to start sinning? That's one reason why we're admonished in 1 Thessalonians 5:17 to "pray continually," or, as the KJV puts it, "Pray without ceasing." But how is that possible? Men, women, boys, and girls have daily lives filled with all sorts of work, instruction, and other activities. Certainly, we cannot keep speaking prayers the entire time we're awake.

Is there actually a means for praying unceasingly amid the demands of daily life? If so, what would that look like for you? How can it be accomplished?

____

____

____

Do you believe you can foster a day-spanning "attitude of prayer"? What do you think an "attitude of prayer" is?

If you begin your day with "Good morning, Holy Spirit" or "Good morning, Father," do you think you could maintain that open connection between the two of you throughout the day? If so, how?

III. Read 1 Peter 5:8–9 and James 4:7.

We are instructed by the apostle Peter and by James, the half-brother of Jesus, to resist the devil. Resistance is the force to remain unmovable—to push back and stand your ground. Between these passages, we find four important elements that we must practice in order to be successful:

1. Be alert and of sober mind.
2. Submit yourself to God.
3. Stand firm in the faith.
4. Resist the devil.

What does it mean to "be alert and of sober mind"? Is it just being aware and having a clear head, or is it more?

"Submit yourself to God" means to give your mind to God and close yourself off to non-beneficial distractions. Is this easy for you? Why or why not?

We are instructed to "stand firm in the faith." How real is your determination to walk out your faith? Explain.

How does one resist an unseen enemy? What weapons might be employed to help?

IV. Read Luke 10:17; Proverbs 18:10; Philippians 2:9–10; Mark 16:17; Luke 10:17; and Hebrews 4:16.

A name? Any name? No. It's *the* Name! The name of our Lord saves the lost. At least three times in the Gospels, Jesus himself said that salvation comes through believing in his name. The apostle John, in 1 John 5:13, stated the same thing about "the name of the Son of God."

The name of Jesus is unlike any other name. His name saves and provides authority to those who have a relationship with him. With it, you can command the enemy to cease, to be quiet, to be cast out, and to leave the scene. In fact, there is much to be learned in the Scriptures about this name.

When you became a Christian, you became an adopted son or daughter of God. You now wear his name and have all the rights, titles, and authority that come with it. How does this encourage your faith?

___

___

___

___

"In the name of Jesus . . ." Demons must listen and yield to the spoken name of Jesus, if the individual speaking it has a relationship with Jesus. Have you ever used his name to take authority over an enemy or situation? If so, briefly describe the experience.

___

___

___

___

There is no biblical evidence that we have authority over angels to "dispatch" them to our defense against the enemy, but we do know the One who can. And in the name of Jesus we can "approach God's throne of grace with confidence, so that we may receive mercy and find grace to help us in our time of need" (Heb 4:16). Are *you* bold enough to do so?

Wrapping Things Up with a Caution

Spiritual warfare is a powerful tool to be used by Christians when and where there is a need, but it should never become a fixation. Don't look for demons under every rock. Our enemy loves it when we fixate on evil rather than on God; it keeps Christians from being focused on things that really matter, and it causes exhaustion.

Regarding Prayer

Prayer can certainly be done silently, but there can be benefits when done aloud. As a rule of thumb, spiritual warfare should be performed with your voice so the enemy can hear it and be made to comply. Verbalized prayer can be very effective.

Remember Why We're Here

Spiritual warfare isn't for fun; it's performed to accomplish specific results for the kingdom of God. You are not a physical accident, nor are you here today by accident. The enemy's hordes know that; it's one reason they war against humankind. But with the weaponry the Lord has provided, you can experience victories as you soldier on to see lives saved and changed.

The Peace of the Holy Spirit

You can *know* when the enemy has lost yet another fight—you can *know* you've gained a victory—by the peace you experience from the Holy Spirit. You may live in a world at war, but the Holy Spirit doesn't want your heart to *feel* as though you are living in a world at war. God wants his children to know peace that surpasses understanding, and he will provide it. So, when a battle has been won, it's the Holy Spirit who will confirm it. The urgency you've felt will be gone, and a peace will settle within you. See John 14:27; Philippians 4:7; Romans 8:6; Psalm 23:1–3; and Galatians 5:22–23 for some beautiful promises about God's peace.

Closing Prayer

Father, what a life you have in store for us—yes in heaven, but here also. It will not necessarily be a life of wealth, travel, and entertainment, but one of purpose that can help others who are lost join your family. Help us, Lord, to seek first your kingdom. Help us to see needs and meet them. Help us to notice the attacks of enemy and defeat them. And help us to fall more and more in love with you each day. In Jesus' name, Amen.■